STUDENT-LED DISCUSSIONS

How do I promote rich conversations about books, videos, and other media?

Sandi
NOVAK

 Alexandria, VA USA

ASCD®
Website: www.ascd.org
E-mail: books@ascd.org

ASCD | arias™
www.ascdarias.org

Printed in the United States of America. Cover art © 2014 by ASCD. ASCD publications present a variety of viewpoints. The views expressed or implied in this book should not be interpreted as official positions of the Association.

ASCD LEARN TEACH LEAD® and ASCD ARIAS™ are trademarks owned by ASCD and may not be used without permission. All other referenced trademarks are the property of their respective owners.

PAPERBACK ISBN: 978-1-4166-1948-2   ASCD product #SF114069
Also available as an e-book (see Books in Print for the ISBNs).

Library of Congress Cataloging-in-Publication Data
Novak, Sandi, 1953-
  Student-led discussions : how do I promote rich conversations about books, videos, and other media? / Sandi Novak.
    pages cm.
  Includes bibliographical references.
  ISBN 978-1-4166-1948-2 (pbk.)
1. Group work in education. 2. Discussion—Study and teaching. I. Title.
  LB1032.N68 2014
  371.3'6—dc23
                                                         2014021171

21 20 19 18 17 16 15 14   1 2 3 4 5 6 7 8 9 10

STUDENT-LED DISCUSSIONS

How do I promote rich conversations about books, videos, and other media?

Want to earn a free ASCD Arias e-book?
Your opinion counts! Please take 2–3 minutes to give
us your feedback on this publication. All survey
respondents will be entered into a drawing to
win an ASCD Arias e-book.

Please visit
www.ascd.org/ariasfeedback

Thank you!

Introduction

The 6th grade lesson began like any other typical classroom activity; the teacher told the students they were going to compare and contrast different texts and genres to understand their approaches to similar themes and topics. However, what happened next differed from what is typically found in many middle school classrooms.

Students gathered in groups of four or five and began to discuss the anchor prompt while using other questions they had generated after reading three books: *Iqbal*, *Wonder*, and *The Hunger Games*. The conversation flowed fluidly with all students participating and asking questions such as, "How would you compare Iqbal in *Iqbal* to August in *Wonder*?" "What do you think is worse for August: the bullying because of his face or just the fact that he has a different face?" and "Who do you think experienced more social injustice, Iqbal in *Iqbal*, August in *Wonder*, or Katniss in *The Hunger Games*?" These questions were generated by students of varying abilities, and all members were eager to contribute to the group discussion. Even though not all of the questions were formed properly, they represented the deep thinking students had done on their own.

After this discussion, one of the students, Haroon, shared with his teacher that *Wonder* was the first chapter book he had read completely on his own. When asked why he chose to read this book, he responded matter-of-factly: "All of my friends in the group were reading and talking about the book, and it sounded interesting. So I wanted to read it too. But it was hard for me. I had to sit with a dictionary next to me and look up words I didn't know. At first, I had to look up a lot of words, but as we talked about the book, it got easier to read."

We've known for almost 20 years that student-led discussions result in better outcomes. So why aren't these practices seen in more classrooms across the country? The most common response given by educators is that students don't take responsibility when teacher-led questioning strategies are used; therefore, teachers don't believe students will be ready to do it on their own.

This publication seeks to provide educators with a framework that describes what some teachers have done to help students experience the type of success exemplified by Haroon and his classmates. In addition, I hope to offer K–12 educators a resource to use when teaching students to engage in rich conversations about books, video, or other media. Finally, I'll share how to gradually release responsibility to students when they are able to conduct effective and productive conversations on their own.

The perspective presented in the following pages takes conversations to a deeper level and should be used in all disciplines. *Student-Led Discussions* provides a basis for dialogue across all grades and content areas. Although prescriptions for how to teach are not provided, a number of written examples and codes for video viewing are included to demonstrate students' thinking and show examples of key discussion components across grades. Throughout, there are video references to help clarify written text and show authentic examples of student work. A number of video clips with their respective links will appear in specific places throughout these pages to provide vivid, visual examples in order to add more clarity to the content. Additionally, a complete list of all the videos is listed in the Encore section.

To aid comprehension, I recommend you read the text in its entirety before viewing the video examples. After you finish reading and understand the flow and content of the ideas presented, you can reread sections of interest before viewing the related videos.

The students in these videos did not follow a script or practice prior to capturing these examples. Occasionally, you may see other students or hear surrounding classroom noise, which further demonstrates the authenticity of the work. To eliminate background noise in most examples, small groups of students were taken to other quiet areas of the school during the recording.

Videos of students in 1st through 9th grades were selected for this resource. Although the context and level of discussion may differ, many of the underlying themes and core elements are appropriate for students from the primary grades through high school.

It takes a long time to develop a classroom culture of self-directed learners in which deep, rich conversations flow seamlessly among students. I hope that *Student-Led Discussions* provides direction and tools to develop the capacity of your students to lead and engage in extensive discussions that result in more student talk, higher-level thinking, wider group participation, greater group cohesion, and richer inquiry. Nystrand (2006) found that as little as 10 minutes of text-based peer discussion daily improved students' standardized test scores. Students who engage in these types of meaningful conversations will also experience and practice the skills necessary to become productive citizens in the 21st century.

How Do Student-Led Discussions Align with Established Standards?

The content of student-led discussions comes from literary and informational text. Regardless of which set of standards is in place, students are required to read widely and deeply from a broad range of high-quality, increasingly challenging text. Consequently, by reading texts in social studies, science, and other content areas, students are able to build a foundation of knowledge in these subjects that also provides the background necessary to be better readers and problem solvers in all content areas. These anchor standards define the skills and understandings that all students must demonstrate without relying on the teacher to prompt or facilitate the process.

The Speaking and Listening strand of the Common Core State Standards (CCSS) requires students to develop a range of useful communication and interpersonal skills. To become college and career ready, students need ample opportunities to take part in a variety of rich, structured conversations—as part of a whole class, in small groups, and with partners—built around important content in various domains. They need to be taught how to contribute appropriately to these conversations, and they need time to practice. During these conversations, students learn to apply the skills necessary to compare and contrast and to analyze and synthesize a multitude of ideas in accordance with the standards appropriate to a particular discipline. Through student-led discussions, students will enhance their ability to listen attentively so they are able to build on others' ideas while expressing their own ideas clearly and persuasively.

What Classroom Structures Are Needed for Student-Led Discussions?

To facilitate student-led discussions successfully, certain core structures are necessary in any classroom. For example, a classroom environment that focuses on collaboration and the importance of student voice is mandatory to facilitate robust conversations.

Rich, strategy-building discussions don't just happen. Many of the skills needed for great student-led conversations take all year to build, and a foundation needs to be built upon a collaborative climate within the classroom—one established on trust produced by honest, open, consistent, and respectful behavior. Within such a climate, groups perform well; without it, they fail. Teachers need to set, model, and monitor high standards that are understood by all students. In addition, group members need to know what is expected of them both individually and collectively.

All too often, students are not given enough opportunities to listen to others, respond and construct ideas, respectfully challenge others' ideas, and respond to challenges to their own ideas without teacher support and facilitation. Students who participate in these kinds of targeted conversations are better able to examine, scrutinize, challenge, validate, and shape the ideas being discussed. Through this process, students become consumers of information with the skills necessary for future success.

In many classrooms, though, opportunities for students to talk about text are limited to the learning of facts and procedures rather than discussing and deepening understandings. Students are capable of so much more. Teachers need to cultivate opportunities for students to apply their learning to their discussions. Usually, when discussion breaks down within groups, it's because students have not been properly trained in effective, productive group expectations, norms, and responsibilities.

Diverse perspectives need to be respected and encouraged. In order to foster an environment in which multiple perspectives are encouraged, it is important for teachers to promote, model, and assess each student's involvement.

This structure should always follow the same framework:

1. Deliver a focus lesson of no more than 15 or 20 minutes, during which you explicitly teach, model, and provide guided practice of important content or processes.

2. Encourage students to apply new techniques within student-led discussions.

3. Observe and record data about individual students' contributions and overall group behavior.

4. Provide feedback on students' application of the areas of focus and other content and process skills.

5. Have students reflect on the day's lesson, their individual contributions, and how their groups functioned.

Meaningful discussions that are more student-focused and rely less on the teacher require explicit instruction and practice using focus lessons to ensure students' success. A focus lesson is a short lesson used to teach particular skills, introduce strategies, extend previous learning, or create interest in a topic. During a focus lesson, only one strategy, skill, or concept should be taught. Teachers introduce the topic; demonstrate the strategy, skill, or concept; guide student practice; discuss the topic; volunteer other possible examples; and talk about what was taught. At the end of a focus lesson, teachers discuss how the process might be applied to students' own discussions and outline what they'll be looking for during their observations.

Growth in meaningful discussions has a cumulative influence on reading, writing, speaking, and listening. Therefore, explicit instruction through the use of focus lessons should occur at each grade level. Within each focus lesson, students need to be given opportunities to practice the new skill with guidance prior to practicing on their own. The early stages of learning are critical in determining future success because initial errors can become ingrained and difficult to fix. Therefore, students' initial attempts at new strategies and skills should be carefully monitored and, when necessary, guided so they are accurate and successful.

After the focus lesson, students should get together in small groups to practice the task. Your role as teacher is to move among the groups, taking notes and offering assistance if discussion breaks down. Be careful not to jump in and offer advice if there is just a lull in the conversation. Some struggle is necessary for students to develop and become self-directed learners.

The amount of time allocated to student-led discussions may vary depending on the grade level and students' ages; however, all group discussions should begin with less time and gradually add time as students' stamina develops. Generally speaking, when their stamina is fully developed, 20–30 minutes is often sufficient for good, rich, deep discussions to take place. Given too much time, conversations may drift off topic or there may not be enough time for feedback and reflection to occur.

After students feel a certain amount of comfort and familiarity with the strategy taught in the focus lesson, groups may self-assess by using a checklist of desired outcomes. This reflection provides time for students to think about what worked well and what needs more practice to become effective. The middle and high school checklist in the Encore section (p. 46) provides a comprehensive list of attributes that students will need to use when they engage in effective discussions. When used for instructional purposes, attributes listed on a checklist should be limited to a workable number of new elements along with a few items that have been applied and assessed previously.

Prompts for Reflective Dialogue:

- What general characteristics exist in environments where student-led discussions flourish?
- What is the leader's (e.g., principal or department chair) responsibility in helping to ensure student-led discussions are practiced in all classrooms?
- What strategies and skills need to be taught explicitly in each grade in order to foster student-led discussions?

What Core Elements Are Needed for Students to Engage in Rich Discussions?

Purpose. Significant discussions happen for a reason, yet the purpose is often not clear to students. As students begin to engage in meaningful discussions, they need to know if they are exploring ideas, expanding their understanding of an important topic, solving a problem, or debating a position. The text that will be used—along with questions, prompts, or wonderings—will help shape and focus a productive conversation.

Text selection. Students should have some choice in the assigned texts, and that material should be appropriate for their reading level. Just like other instruction, it is important to begin with tightly structured controls and move toward more freedom of text selection as students demonstrate their personal responsibility and gain knowledge of rituals, routines, and expectations. Therefore, teachers often limit students' ability to choose texts to just two selections at the beginning of the year. As students experience more and more success with their discussions and are able to apply information from the focus lessons, the number of choices they are offered may expand by several titles. When students have choice in what they read, they are more motivated to read (Allington & Gabriel, 2012) and engage in deeper, more thoughtful discussions (Zwiers & Crawford, 2011).

Group membership and communication skills. Group membership skills required for meaningful discussion include understanding one's role and responsibilities and being an effective listener, contributor, and group member. Many communication skills are taken for granted in schools, yet they are not automatic in all students. Skills such as listening attentively, using paraphrasing for clarification, and turn-taking evolve through seeing effective examples, practicing, and receiving specific feedback. All students can benefit from explicit instruction and opportunities to apply these and other communication and social skills.

Manners, behaviors, and nonverbal signals are also important. Many students—especially English language learners (ELLs) and students who have not been immersed in communication at home—will improve their skills once they are exposed to effective modeling and given time to practice in the classroom. We cannot assume students will automatically make appropriate eye contact, have attentive posture, and listen without interrupting when they engage in classroom conversations. All of these skills will need to be modeled and practiced explicitly. When students practice these skills, and when teachers provide specific feedback to individuals or groups, the likelihood of them regularly using these behaviors and skills correctly increases and soon becomes part of their repertoire.

Discussion-worthy questions and prompts. When teachers first introduce students to the idea of having their own conversations, they often provide the questions and prompts themselves. However, this responsibility—generating higher-level questions, wonderings, and prompts—should be released to students as soon as they are ready.

Once students have been trained to come up with conversation-worthy questions about a text or topic, they can measure their questions against criteria such as "Does this question allow for several different perspectives that will engage other students in a deep conversation?" or "Is this prompt something you would find interesting enough to talk about with your friends for an extended period of time?" These leading questions help students analyze their own questions to determine if those questions will help focus a conversation while also allowing for deep discussion around an important topic.

Need-based focus areas. Sometimes the strengths and needs of individual students determine the content or process skills to address within the whole group. As you observe students during their discussions, they will undoubtedly demonstrate strengths in some areas while other areas of need bubble to the surface. Often, the best focus lessons stem from students telling the teacher when they got stuck in a particular area or from the teacher noting common struggles within groups. Through sensitive observation, you can decide which specific strategies to foster among your students.

For example,

- Students who don't participate in or know what to say during a conversation should get into the habit of writing prepared notes. Eventually, it will become second nature to search various information sources to identify and obtain key concepts they can use to contribute to class discussions.

- Students who are able to develop ideas but never disagree or challenge other's ideas need to learn how to evaluate differing points of view critically and constructively.

- A particular group may demonstrate strength in its ability to pose and respond to specific questions with elaboration and detail by making comments that contribute to the topic, text, or issue under discussion, but members aren't able to close the conversation by synthesizing important points. In this case, the teacher would provide targeted feedback to the group and make a note on his or her recording sheet.

For any of these examples (and many more), if similar observations are noted among multiple groups, then the relevant skill should become the topic of the next focus lesson. By listening and keeping good notes of individual and group skills, an attentive teacher is able to make informed decisions about specific strategies or skills to focus on and foster among students.

While students practice applying new techniques in their group discussions, it's a good idea to post or hang anchor charts, sentence stems, and sample words around the classroom for students to use when communication stalls. However, relying too much on these prompts can prohibit effective and natural conversation, especially if students need to search for support structures whenever they speak. Therefore, by using the gradual release of responsibility model (Pearson & Gallagher, 1983), this support should be slowly phased out after students demonstrate success.

Conversation roles. In some classrooms, teachers assign group membership roles to students (e.g., note taker, facilitator, time keeper), whereas in other classrooms students engage in conversations without having assigned responsibilities. After observing many conversations using a variety of different approaches, it has become apparent that conversations flow more fluidly and are more in-depth if all students are familiar with the various roles up front and grow, through practice, to accept responsibility for any role. Roles may certainly be assigned when students are first learning about student-led discussions and when you're reinforcing the differences among them, but the ultimate goal is to have students become knowledgeable of each role and be able to assume any one of them as the need arises.

Opportunities to challenge other perspectives. For many ELLs and students whose home life does not provide sufficient oral language stimulation, student-led classroom discussions immerse them in an environment prime for developing ideas and language skills. Unfortunately, many students are rarely exposed to enough examples of appropriate confrontation and persuasion skills. Through explicit teaching and opportunities to practice these communication skills, students can be provided with a productive way to handle conflict—one that teaches them how to respectfully challenge another person's idea or to respond to challenges of their own ideas without becoming argumentative, defensive, or explosive. Students quickly learn that *what* they say and *how* they say it are powerful means of communication and that it's possible to disagree with someone while still maintaining and respecting that person's dignity and respect.

Let's consider an example. Two 1st grade students are comparing and contrasting two books. One student made a statement, and the other's facial expression looked surprised. The listener then challenges the speaker by quietly saying "No" in disagreement. The speaker doesn't know how to respond. By contrast, two 2nd grade students who have had opportunities to challenge and be challenged by different perspectives are discussing the similarities and differences between two versions of *The Three Little Pigs.* One girl makes a statement her partner questions, and the former quickly jumps into action and opens the text to show evidence of her claim, which convinces her partner that her claim is accurate.

Students in all grades can be taught how to criticize ideas constructively, consider well-supported points, question the quality of various claims, and make joint decisions. Some of the best learning opportunities involve negotiating opposing viewpoints. Indeed, sharing ideas, defending positions, and making connections use the tools of language in ways that can influence others while cultivating one's own language skills.

Clear areas of focus. Sometimes teachers prefer to demonstrate the particular skills necessary for rich discussion by making the process more visible. To accomplish this goal, some teachers elect to use a Socratic Seminar model. A Socratic Seminar begins with a question that is either posed by the leader or solicited from participants. An opening question has no right answer; instead, it reflects a genuine curiosity on the part of the questioner. In a Socratic Seminar, the leader demonstrates processes that lead to thoughtful exploration of ideas by keeping the discussion focused, asking follow-up questions, helping participants clarify their positions when arguments become confused, and involving reluctant participants while restraining their more vocal peers.

Typically, students read a text selection and then form two concentric circles. The inner circle examines and discusses the text while the second circle comments on the quality of the dialogue. Then the two circles reverse roles, and the process is repeated.

Socratic circles are one way for teachers to relinquish some (but not all!) control by partially turning it over to students. This method encourages students to work cooperatively to construct meaning from what they have read, practice various discussion techniques, and avoid focusing on a "correct" interpretation of the text.

The drawbacks of this method are that—in a typical classroom—the two concentric circles are generally quite large, which may limit participation, and the facilitation of the process is often led by the teacher. These limitations do not escalate to concerns unless students rarely have occasions to work in pairs, triads, or small groups where their full participation and chances to take responsibility for their learning intensify. Students benefit when given ample opportunities to take part in a variety of rich, structured conversations—as part of a large group, in small groups, and with partners.

New vocabulary words. The National Institute of Child Health and Human Development (2000) advocates direct vocabulary instruction as an effective instructional method for students' reading comprehension. However, not all practice is equally effective.

Marzano and Pickering (2005) offer a process for teaching new terms that help students gain an understanding of meaning by providing an explanation of each new term, rewriting the definition in their own words, engaging in activities that help them add to their knowledge about the new term, and discussing the new term with one another.

Despite these recommendations, students rarely have the opportunity or incentive to play around with and use new words in their conversations. When they do, the exercise typically revolves around the traditional approach of reciting a new word and its definition. Students need to see good models of how to use vocabulary words when they talk with one another about a text.

Note-taking. Writing (for older students) and drawing pictures (for younger students) are important strategies to capture students' thinking about text. While reading, students can use sticky notes or response logs to help them remember key elements they will later bring to the discussion. After a focus lesson is taught, students often use their notes and background knowledge during their discussions to prompt the application of this dedicated skill or concept.

Likewise, when a teacher observes a discussion, it is a natural opportunity to assess the progress of both individual students and the larger group. There are many different ways teachers can take observational notes, but it is important for student growth to jot down your important thoughts, students' success at learning content, and students' use of communication and social skills. These notes will help you understand how students are reading, thinking, and interacting. As you notice patterns develop, you have a strong foundation to coach individual students privately, and when patterns become more widespread, they can serve as the topic of future focus lessons.

Reflection. Hammond and Nessel (2011) discuss and provide some benefits of peer interaction that are directly related to comprehension. One benefit is that interaction improves students' capacities for thinking: "As students learn to weigh each other's contributions, they become more discerning and more adept at thinking" (p. 88). After each discussion, it is important for students to reflect on the things they learned and the contributions they made. This reflection can be done orally or in writing through the use of a journal. Conversations are useful for assessing how students use the knowledge they have learned as they work with others to negotiate and construct ideas.

Prompts for Reflective Dialogue:
- What other core elements are important to explicitly teach, model, and have students practice?

- Which of the core elements will you teach first?
- How do the core skills differ among grade levels?

How Do I Get Started as a 1st–3rd Grade Teacher?

Higher-achieving students "spent 70 percent of their instructional time reading passages and discussing or responding to questions about the material they read. In contrast, lower-achieving readers spent roughly 37 percent of their instructional time on these activities. The majority of their time was spent on word-identification, letter-sound activities, spelling and penmanship" (Allington, 2001, p. 25).

Children in the early grades benefit from participating in rich, structured conversation in response to books that are read aloud by an adult or an older, more fluent reader. Meaning-making is enhanced when teachers talk about text and provide students with opportunities to share their thinking, questions, and feelings.

Student-led discussions in the early grades offer pairs or triads of readers the opportunity to engage in conversations about, deepen their understanding of, and share their interpretations of texts.

So, are these early learners capable of having student-led discussions about text?

In short, yes! They are absolutely capable of beginning conversations about text read aloud by the teacher or from books appropriate to their reading level. In the early grades, students will be most successful when they begin this work in pairs.

Support is especially important for young learners as they begin the process of having conversations about text with partners or in triads. To help these students get started, text frames and anchor charts are structures they need to grow their conversation skills.

Student-led discussions require a great deal of teacher support at the beginning, but with careful planning and explicit instruction, students can become more independent in this work. In the beginning, the teacher often selects texts that will be of interest to students and that allow them the ability to apply an appropriate comprehension strategy from the focus lesson.

In the primary grades, students who will be working together should read the same texts. As students become more skilled, they can be encouraged to read and discuss books by the same author or books that are based on a common topic. Since picture books and early chapter books are generally short in length, children typically read the whole book before they have a discussion rather than reading shorter sections and having several discussions (i.e., like older students who read longer books).

What do early readers talk about when they begin working independently in pairs and triads? The focus of their discussions can be on sharing new information they learned;

describing things they liked (or didn't like) about the book; asking questions they had before, during, or after reading; sharing new reading strategies; discussing the notes they took while reading to keep track of their thinking and questions; or using charts and mind maps to compare characters and ideas.

In a 1st grade classroom, the teacher can provide a focus lesson on asking and answering questions while he or she reads a story. Students draw pictures, write keywords, or write full questions (if able) on sticky notes as they generate their questions about the text. When they finish, they reread their questions and silently use their sticky notes as a guide. Later, in pairs, the partners ask and answer each other's questions without assistance from the teacher. (See Video 3: Discussion, Grade 1: Asking and Answering Questions.)

You might be thinking to yourself that this is not an example of discussion. And you're right! Conversation is much more than simply talking and listening; it requires incremental steps, explicit instruction, and lots of practice to get all students willingly engaged in deep, meaningful conversations about text. In the previous example, the incremental steps include having students write questions on sticky notes, practice the questions on their own, and then ask their questions to a partner. By writing down their questions as they read, students are better able to organize their thoughts before sharing them with a partner. In this particular lesson, these 1st grade students participate in collaborative conversations by listening to others with care, speaking one at a time, and asking and answering questions with a partner in order to gather additional information or clarify something.

After several lessons aimed at guiding students' developmental progress, they receive explicit instruction on how to compare and contrast two texts and engage in a conversation on their own. Again, the first time they practice on their own does not result in a true "conversation." One student mentions something about one text, and the other student responds by noting a similarity or difference in the other text. However, these beginning lessons and opportunities to practice are crucial to students' success as they develop their independence (See Video 4: Discussion, Grade 1: Comparing and Contrasting.)

Let's consider another example. A 2nd grade teacher sets the following learning target for a lesson: identify one similarity and one difference between two stories. She begins the gradual release of responsibility model by having students compare and contrast a soccer and basketball. They construct a Venn diagram and work in groups to identify and add similarities and differences. The focus lesson takes about 20 minutes for the teacher to provide direction, for students to generate similarities and differences on chart paper, and for students to share their ideas. (See Video 5: Focus Lesson, Grade 2: Comparing and Contrasting.) Although students might have opportunities to practice writing questions and answers, it's more than likely that they do not have similar opportunities to be part of productive conversations with one another.

The day before, the teacher read a traditional version of the Little Red Riding Hood tale along with a much different interpretation—*Honestly, Red Riding Hood Was Rotten: The Story of Little Red Riding Hood as told by the Wolf* (Shaskan & Guerlais, 2011). After the teacher finished reading, students listed one similarity and one difference between the two stories on sticky notes. Finally, the teacher had the students share their ideas. This lesson was taught to lead up to the work students would do to compare and contrast two or more versions of the same story by different authors (CCSS. ELA-Literacy.RL.2.9).

This preparatory work can be approached differently, but all students must be afforded multiple opportunities to acquire the skills necessary to meet the standard. In another 2nd grade classroom, the teacher might present a number of focus lessons leading up to the culminating activity of comparing and contrasting several versions of the Three Little Pigs folktale. Although the stories used to teach this standard are different, both classes are introduced to and practice multiple relevant skills before focusing on the standard. In short, both teachers provide focus lessons on asking and answering questions while reading and listening carefully to a partner as he or she speaks.

After several focus lessons and opportunities to discuss texts, students are set to work independently to compare and contrast different texts and have a conversation about the similarities and differences. In both examples, students can be asked to use the information they placed on their graphic organizers to have a conversation about the two versions of the folktale they read. Remember that it's critical for the teacher to model a good conversation and remind students of the qualities of a good conversation.

When students are engaged in these conversations, the teacher walks around with a list of indicators (shared and discussed with students earlier), noting specific examples he or she will share with students later in the lesson. This type of data collection and feedback should be given at the end of each lesson for students to make necessary adjustments in how they conduct and interact during discussions. (See Video 6: Discussion, Grade 2: Comparing and Contrasting.)

Even though all students may not be able to meet the various mandated standards at a proficient level, many experience great growth and success when they are afforded opportunities to practice strategies independently. In addition, their communication skills can only develop through structured practice with specific feedback from the teacher. Most importantly, their love of reading increases with each opportunity to practice and communicate about high-quality, rich literature.

Prompts for Reflective Dialogue:
- What strategies could be taught to support students in the primary grades as they work toward independence in their conversations about texts?
- What skills do primary students need in order to move from having conversations about texts with a partner to working in triads and small groups?

- How do conversations strengthen skills for all students in the primary grades?

What Do Student-Led Discussions Look Like in Grades 4 and 5?

In Danielson's (2007) rubric of using questioning and discussion techniques, a teacher is designated as *distinguished* when students assume considerable responsibility for the success of the discussion, initiate topics, and make unsolicited contributions. To be classified in this category, all students need to engage in highly functioning group discussions, all students' perspectives should be encouraged, and all voices need to be heard. Rather than the teacher guiding conversations and leading discussions, students assume considerable responsibility for the depth and breadth of the dialogue. Ultimately, students themselves ensure high levels of participation.

Daniels (2002) notes that a "natural home" for text discussions is in the intermediate grades. Many teachers have made progress in identifying and teaching comprehension strategies such as predicting, inferring, questioning, and making connections. However, it takes deeper thinking to apply these comprehension strategies while conversing about text; all too often, the strategies used to communicate effectively in group discussions are not explicitly taught and modeled.

Let's take a look at a scenario. A 5th grade teacher provides a focus lesson and has students practice the skill of building on other group members' ideas. At first, students rely on cue cards that hang from the ceiling to confirm that the speaker had been understood. Students in one group exhibit effective communication skills when they connect what was said to other ideas by saying things such as "I agree," "As Emma was saying . . . ," and "How does that relate to your life?" Later, they speak with confidence, and the conversation thrives without the use of additional supports as they discuss the assigned text. (See Video 8: Discussion, Grade 5: Communication Skills.)

One student describes the symbolic relationship between an object in the current text and a different object in a previously assigned book. This type of sophisticated connection between objects in two different texts exposes other students to advanced language and thinking skills that may be unlike their own. Making connections and drawing parallels may not be natural to some students, or they may not have much practice using examples to support their ideas. Therefore, one of the greatest gifts we can give students is the set of skills needed to productively and effectively collaborate in meaningful discussions with others.

If we want students to experience great success with student-led discussions, it's important to teach a number of focus lessons on ways to enhance discussions and keep students on topic. Some appropriate topics include staying focused, allowing all group members several opportunities to speak, extending ideas, working together as a team, assuming different roles within the group, using text evidence to support ideas, and summarizing points a speaker makes. Besides explicitly teaching and modeling these things, it's critical to extend opportunities for students to practice during dedicated class discussion time. (See Video 7: Focus Lesson, Grade 5: Citing Text Evidence.)

Now let's take a look at a 4th grade example. The teacher wants her focus lesson to be on comparing and contrasting two characters in different novels. She sets up a Socratic Seminar and has the students sit in two concentric circles. She first models her thinking about a few similarities and differences between two identified characters by using a Venn diagram. Then she asks students in the inner circle to have a conversation about other similarities and differences while students in the outer circle take notes so they can provide feedback after the conversation.

Finally, the students in the outer circle provide feedback followed by the teacher's contributions of her own observations. For example, a student mentioned that one character felt great joy at a particular point in the story and demonstrated that joy by dancing around. That student also suggested that he didn't think the character in the other story felt the same joy. With this in mind, the teacher prompts the group with questions that guide them to consider whether the other character displayed similar emotions or had similar feelings.

Rather than telling students how her point of view differs from theirs regarding the two characters' experiences with joy, she poses questions. By using this instructional technique, she allows students to reflect on their own thinking and learning, and she demonstrates through modeling that each student is responsible for his or her own learning. This instructional technique helps build a collaborative environment while ensuring every student's voice is valued. (See Video 9: Focus Lesson, Grade 4: Grand Conversation.)

Professional organizations recommend this type of instruction: more experiential, inductive, hands-on learning; a greater emphasis on higher-order thinking; more responsibility transferred to students for their work; and more cooperative, collaborative activity that develops the classroom into an interdependent community (Thompson & Zueli, 1999).

Prompts for Reflective Dialogue:
- What do student-led discussions look like when the process is implemented well?
- What is the role of the teacher when students are involved in leading their own discussions?
- What are the most challenging skills used in discussions, and how can a teacher instruct students to use these skills effectively?

How Can the Process Be Used with Middle and High School Students?

By the middle and high school levels, students are able to read a wide assortment of books around common themes and have discussions with the purpose of gaining a wider perspective of topics. Sometimes students benefit from being in discussions with other students who read the same information, whereas at other times their skills are enhanced when they meet in groups where students have read different texts around a common theme. (See Video 10: Discussion, Grade 6: Asking Good Questions.)

Although the use of open-ended questions is extremely important to rich conversations, the true value of student-led discussions occurs when students engage in deep dialogue around big ideas and are able to extend and clarify their thoughts about a discipline, a topic, or the world. When students are exposed to focus lessons that progress from asking relevant questions to citing textual evidence to digging deep into concepts, they are able to refine and negotiate their thoughts while challenging one another to use more advanced language and thinking skills. Zwiers & Crawford (2011) indicate that such conversations provide opportunities to understand and create ideas, values, biases, perspectives, and purposes. (See Video 11: Discussion, Grade 6: Big Ideas.)

Let's look at a real-life 6th grade example to explain this concept more thoroughly. To teach the concept of social justice, a 6th grade teacher assigned one book—*Bud, Not Buddy* by Christopher Paul Curtis—as a resource she had all students read. This was the anchor text. She then used book talks to provide motivation and some background information about other books students could read on the same topic—*Wonder* by R.J. Palacio, *Iqbal* by Francesco D'Adamo, *The Hunger Games* by Suzanne Collins, *Out of My Mind* by Sharon Draper, and *Kizzy Ann Stamps* by Jeri Watts. During the focus lesson, the teacher focused on evaluating group members' use of evidence. To that end, she provided a good and not-so-good example as part of the modeling step. She used the picture book *Sit In: How Four Friends Stood Up by Sitting Down* by Andrea Davis Pinkney and said, "The author uses a repeated pattern in several places within the text: 'All they wanted was some food. A doughnut and coffee, with cream on the side.' Having a doughnut and coffee seems so normal, routine, and carefree, yet these four African American students were breaking tradition by sitting at a 'Whites Only' lunch counter. This group of sentences used throughout the book contributes to the development of the central message about four college students staging a peaceful protest."

After the teacher provided this example, students used a 1–5 scale to rate how effectively the evidence aligned with the concept she wanted to convey. Though it is important to provide effective examples, it is also important to provide less-effective examples for students to deepen and broaden their understanding. To demonstrate a weak example, the teacher used the same picture book where the evidence didn't match the concept she wanted to highlight. After she modeled these two examples of using evidence when conveying a message, she asked students to determine the elements used when supporting an idea, perspective, or argument with text or media.

After completing the social justice unit, this 6th grade teacher taught a three-week unit of study on children's lives around the world. Throughout the unit, students read, discussed, compared, and analyzed various resources related to the topic. As students read a text, they would write and share their thoughts with a partner. Then they would explain what they had learned from each resource. Discussions took place in pairs, triads, and groups of varying sizes. As each new text was added, students spent considerable time comparing and contrasting that piece with those previously read. The culminating activity was a discussion during which students compared and contrasted texts from different genres—*Iqbal,* a novel written by Fancesco D'Adamo; *Mosetsana,* a poem written by Katie Pepiot; *The Negro Mother,* a poem written by Langston Hughes; *From the Shacks to the Prom,* a poem about a South African girl's night of glamour; and various video clips.

When examining the conversation skills required for these activities, it is apparent that students were able to apply information acquired through focus lessons taught throughout the year. (See Video 11: Discussion, Grade 6: Big Ideas.) During their student-led discussions, students were able to

- Develop big ideas.
- Elaborate and clarify.
- Support ideas with examples.
- Paraphrase.
- Synthesize.

When this 6th grade teacher wanted to teach and have students practice citing textual evidence, she spent about two weeks delivering focus lessons on this skill to support analysis of what a text says explicitly as well as inferences that can be drawn from it. To provide examples, she referred to an anchor text that all students had read. She provided the initial prompt in the form of a question to get the conversation started. After the focus lesson, students spent a few minutes gathering examples from the text by writing them in their response logs before meeting and practicing in small groups with others who had read the same text. While in their discussion groups, they asked questions and used examples of textual evidence to keep the conversation flowing.

Throughout the following two weeks, students continued to practice this skill, but the focus lessons went into more depth. For example, the teacher demonstrated how to use relevant evidence to support points when speaking and how to make your reasoning clear to other group members. Again, the examples she used came from the common anchor text, and students were given opportunities to practice in their small groups. Other focus lessons continued to build with more detailed information.

Key concepts of subsequent focus lessons included the following

- Evaluating other group members' use of evidence.
- Absorbing, understanding, and considering ideas and points of view from other group members without debating and arguing every point.
- Comprehending and evaluating texts in order to construct effective arguments and convey intricate or multifaceted information.
- Evaluating other points of view critically and constructively.
- Discerning a group member's key points, requesting clarification, and asking relevant follow-up questions to keep the discussion flowing.

What happens when discussions get stuck? One 9th grade Language Arts teacher used a Socratic Seminar to facilitate student-led discussions and make their practice more visible since students were having difficulty citing textual evidence during discussions. The teacher posed a question to get the conversation started and then instructed students in the inner circle to talk to one another about it. She encouraged each to contribute to the discussion while focusing on four relevant skills: responding to the anchor question, elaborating on another student's question or idea, asking additional open-ended questions, and citing evidence from the text. (See Video 13: Fishbowl Discussion, Grade 9: Citing Evidence.)

During this discussion, the teacher and the students in the outer circle took notes so they could provide feedback to their classmates. After the feedback was provided, the teacher released students to practice the skill in their book clubs. This additional small-group practice afforded more students with the opportunity to practice their skills. The more opportunities students have to practice, the better they become at asking good questions, engaging in deep discussion, and harnessing their communication and social skills.

In a 7th grade classroom, students were asked to find new vocabulary words in a text they were reading, predict their meaning, look up the definitions in a dictionary, and then incorporate the new words into their discussions. During one discussion, students reported on the meaning of words such as *stragglers, sarcasm, vaulting,* and *cavern.* They used these words in authentic discourse, which required them to use variations of each word throughout the discussion. For example, when a student talked about sarcasm, he needed to also use the word *sarcastic.*

When students used these new words in slightly different ways, they stretched their personal vocabularies, which made the words easier to remember in the future. During their discussion, students went beyond just reporting on the meaning of the new words. They asked questions such as "What is the most important word?" and "Which word is important to the story?" (See Video 12: Discussion, Grade 7: Vocabulary.)

Bakhtin (1986) suggested that we learn words not from dictionaries but from other people; words carry with them the accumulated meanings of their previous users. The discussion that transpired around the new words was incredibly effective at helping students master the vocabulary—much more so than simply studying words and meanings for a vocabulary quiz. This authentic discourse is vital to lasting learning. Even though explicit vocabulary instruction is necessary to help students access difficult text and concepts, students will not become independently adept at vocabulary acquisition until they develop an innate ability to know what to do with new and unfamiliar words.

The goal is for students to act as proficient readers by making decisions about words instead of becoming dependent on teachers to put words on vocabulary lists. Rather than seeing a set of vocabulary words on a list developed by a teacher as an end point of learning, productive and engaging discussions help students simultaneously learn the vocabulary and develop their thinking skills.

Prompts for Reflective Dialogue:
- What types of student-led discussions are most successful with adolescents and young adults?
- How can student-led discussions help students understand content, develop communication skills, and cultivate social interactions?
- Which content and skills will be most successfully taught and practiced through the use of student-led discussions?

How Can the Process Be Used in Subjects Other Than Language Arts?

In a 9th grade social studies classroom, students are studying and discussing current issues in Eastern Europe and the Middle East. Over the course of several weeks, students identify and follow the issues developing in those areas. To prepare for their discussion, students are instructed to find and read at least four online articles from credible sources and view at least two videos. Even though not all students read and watched the same information, they all brought common knowledge about the topic to the discussion.

During the unit, a rapidly escalating crisis develops in real time in that region of the world. In order to have a conversation that discusses possible solutions to the crisis, students need to understand the history of the region and the events that precipitated the current event and apply many different thinking skills. For example, as part of a productive student-led discussion, the following thinking skills should be evident: analyzing the situation, making comparisons, understanding cause and effect, problem solving, persuading, empathizing, interpreting, evaluating, and synthesizing. (See Video 14: Social Studies, Grade 9.)

Through this process, students not only experience an opportunity for deep cognitive thought but also enjoy the experience. When high school students talk about the types of teaching they respond to, they "describe their preferred instructional strategies as ones that are hands-on and that contain opportunities for debate and discussion" (Certo, Cauley, Moxley, & Chafin, 2008, p. 32).

We often don't know what students understand about important content until we listen to their conversations. It is when we listen and observe students talking about previously learned principles and laws of science that we can recognize their conceptions and misconceptions.

Leading into a unit of study on ecology, a 7th grade science teacher has her students watch a video called *The Story of Stuff*, which is a short animated documentary about the life cycle of material goods. The film is critical of excessive consumerism and promotes sustainability. She then has them read an article about the effects of climate change. Finally, she prepares students for a Socratic Seminar by asking them to circle key words in the article related to ice, extreme weather, and seasons and underline the author's claims and main idea. Referring to a copy of Bloom's Taxonomy and Costa's Levels of Questioning, she asks students to prepare two Level 2 or 3 questions. Once students are given time to prepare for the discussion, they form two concentric circles and begin a discussion about the information they gleaned from the two resources. (See Video 15: Science, Grade 7.)

As the teacher listens and takes notes during the student-led conversation, she notes some uncertainties and some misconceptions. For example, a student says that it is warmer in the south than it is in the north, so if the South

Pole's ice melted, the animals could be transported to the North Pole to survive. Another student mentions that polar bears become dehydrated from a lack of fresh water to drink and goes on to explain about salt water not being suitable for drinking.

Rather than stopping the flow of discussion, the teacher makes notes about the student's misconception about the climates of the poles and students' puzzled reactions to whether polar bears need fresh water to drink. She plans to address these two areas during the debrief time following the discussion.

"Students must learn to authentically observe, inquire, and hypothesize as scientists do. They can learn some science with a book, but real scientific thinking is founded upon observing phenomena, asking questions about it, and thoughtfully hypothesizing answers or ways to get answers. Science is fueled by wonderings and guesses—and students need to engage in such thinking as much as possible. Unfortunately, many texts and tests cannot or do not emphasize these core skills, and therefore are neglected in many science classes. Conversations can help students focus and develop these skills" (Zwiers & Crawford, 2011, p. 170).

Closing Thought

Kevin Silberman, a 9th grade social studies teacher, sums up the experience of using student-led discussions best:

Originally, I had planned to write a number of questions and have students talk about those questions. Then I found out that for students to engage in student-led discussions, they need to develop their own questions and lead their own conversations. I was obviously nervous about how it would turn out, but as I walked around and listened in on their conversations I found them having these rich, in-depth discussions. Normally, I lead these discussions and drive where the conversations go, but by having students lead their own conversations, their topics were going in so many directions. They were getting to things I don't think I would have led them to. It was then that I realized they had so much more knowledge about these current events they studied than I let them express in class. It was hard as a teacher to give up the control, but the results were awesome!

It is not until students construct their own knowledge that true learning occurs. Students will produce incredible results with appropriate, guided instruction and lots of practice. In order to develop their skills, students need opportunities to practice engaging in conversations around meaningful topics based on multiple sources.

David Perkins, Howard University, has been known to say, "Everyday thinking, like ordinary walking, is a natural performance mastered by all. Good thinking, like running the 100-yard dash, is a technical performance. . . . Sprinters have to be taught how to run the 100-yard dash; good thinking is the result of good teaching, which includes much practice." Similar to the ingredients necessary for good thinking, effective student-led discussions require conscious effort, deliberate instruction, structured practice, specific feedback, focused reflection, and a gradual release of control to students.

To give your feedback on this publication and be entered into a drawing for a free ASCD Arias e-book, please visit
www.ascd.org/ariasfeedback

ENCORE

STUDENT-LED DISCUSSIONS

Q What strategies can I use to get students started with conversations?

A Often, the best place to start is to identify a unit that might work well with more student interaction around the text. Then determine the standards and learning targets that will be addressed in the unit, select appropriate resources, determine the focus lessons that will be taught each day, and just begin! The excitement you receive from students may be the motivation you need to sustain your efforts.

Q What can I do for struggling readers and ELLs who cannot read the texts selected?

A Lent (2012) states, "Just because kids can't read doesn't mean they can't think. They may not be able to read fluently, at least in your content area, but they may be more than capable of thinking through complex ideas. You can support these students' understanding in your content area by providing texts they can read while scaffolding understanding and valuing their contributions in discussions and projects" (p. 93).

Struggling readers sometimes become energized by thinking together with others. For example, a 5th grade teacher forms a small group of students who read below grade level. She asks students who are at or above level if they would like to be involved in two groups. If one or two students choose to be included in the group with below-level readers, their role is to keep the conversation going by drawing other students in, generating some thought-provoking questions, and modeling effective facilitation skills.

Q What can I do to motivate students to read the assigned text?

A Access to high-quality books that students actually want to read is the first step in motivating them to read. It's also important to provide students with some choice in what they read, even if the choice is initially limited to just two different selections. Other students discussing texts they enjoy reading is often all the motivation reluctant readers need to get started. When students have access, choice, and opportunities to talk about text, they are more apt to read.

Q How often should students have student-led discussions?

A To develop their ability to engage in meaningful, powerful discussions, students need to practice regularly. Some teachers find time every day for students to engage in some type of discussion—either in pairs, small groups, or a Socratic Seminar—whereas other teachers concentrate on specific units of study at different times throughout the year for these collaborative discussions.

Q How do I determine what focus lessons are important to teach?

A The Common Core State Standards or other states' standards provide good direction and a place to begin. Nevertheless, the standards themselves are very broad. There are at least five broad topics in which students need explicit instruction during focus lessons in order to have deep, meaningful discussions. They are (1) demonstrate independence and effective group behaviors, (2) build strong content knowledge, (3) adapt communication to audience, task, purpose, and content area, (4) comprehend and critique, and (5) value evidence.

Each of these topics needs to be broken down into "bite-size" pieces that will be explicitly taught, modeled, practiced, and provided with feedback. For example, to demonstrate independence and effective group behaviors, students would be instructed in several tasks in order to gain knowledge and expertise. These concepts would be taught individually over the course of the year: treating others in a respectful, supportive manner; demonstrating reliability by coming prepared for group work; becoming fully engaged in the work of the group and not sitting passively on the sidelines; growing as a self-directed learner, effectively seeking out and using resources to assist in the process; conversing, disagreeing, and challenging ideas in order to learn rather than to win or lose; and working to understand all sides and perspectives of a topic.

Q What strategies work best when showing videos of student-led discussions to help students improve their skills?

A When you want to use video as an instructional tool, it often works best if students are first allowed to watch the video in its entirety in order to understand the content before they are asked to watch again with a particular focus. Their comprehension gets interrupted if they need to focus on specific things contained in the video before they have a chance to watch it generally. For example, small groups of students could be assigned to identify specific instances of relevant skills in a video; they would need to support their ideas with evidence from the video by capturing what was specifically said or done. Examples include instances of students constructing effective arguments and conveying intricate and multifaceted information, requesting clarification and asking relevant questions independently, building on others' ideas and articulating their own ideas by using relevant evidence, demonstrating that they are self-directed learners, and communicating and working together in groups.

FIGURE 1: **Primary Grades Checklist**

___ I read the text.

___ I write some questions while I am reading to use later with my group when we talk about the text.

___ I treat other members of my group with respect.

___ I listen to other members of my group talk without interrupting.

___ I ask other members of my group questions about the text.

___ I speak clearly so others can understand.

FIGURE 2: **Middle and High School Checklist**

Demonstrates independence and effective group behaviors

___ Treats others in a respectful, supportive manner

___ Demonstrates reliability by coming prepared for group work

___ Becomes fully engaged in the work of the group and does not sit passively on the sidelines

___ Grows as a self-directed learner, effectively seeking out and using resources to assist in the process

___ Converses, disagrees, and challenges ideas in order to learn rather than to win or lose

___Works to understand all sides and perspectives of the topic

Builds strong content knowledge

___ Reads purposefully and listens attentively to gain both general knowledge and discipline-specific expertise

___ Refines and shares knowledge through writing prepared notes and speaking

___ Seeks to understand other perspectives and cultures through reading and listening

Adapts communication to audience, task, purpose, and content area

___ Expresses thoughts and ideas in a way that others will understand

___ Discerns a group member's key points, requests clarification, and asks relevant follow-up questions to keep the dialogue flowing

___ Builds on other group members' ideas, articulates own ideas, and confirms that the speaker has been understood

___ Adapts communication in relation to audience, task, purpose, and discipline

___ Sets and adjusts purpose for reading, speaking, listening, and language use as warranted by the task

___ Manages personal contributions to the discussion by monitoring personal participation, listening attentively and nonjudgmentally, managing interruptions, balancing talking with listening, and encouraging others who are not contributing

Comprehends and critiques

___ Absorbs, understands, and considers ideas and points of view from other group members without debating and arguing every point

___ Connects ideas from another group member through the use of paraphrasing or summarizing

___ Comprehends and evaluates texts in order to construct effective arguments and convey intricate or multifaceted information

___ Bases arguments on the content of ideas and opinions and offers opposing views, respectively

___ Evaluates other points of view critically and constructively

FIGURE 2: **Middle and High School Checklist** (*continued*)

Values evidence

___ Cites specific evidence when offering an interpretation of a text

___ Uses relevant evidence to support own points when speaking and making reasoning clear to other group members

___ Evaluates other group members' use of evidence

Video Representations of Student-Led Discussions

	Description	Link
1	Focus Lesson, Grade 1: Asking and Answering Questions	http://youtu.be/UIHU9Jz_smg
2	Feedback, Grade 2	http://youtu.be/OjR5fIy4HmM
3	Discussion, Grade 1: Asking and Answering Questions	http://youtu.be/87Ar2WPxczQ
4	Discussion, Grade 1: Comparing and Contrasting	http://youtu.be/-r4tfcQtX3A
5	Focus Lesson, Grade 2: Comparing and Contrasting	http://youtu.be/1m2DnvIX17I
6	Discussion, Grade 2: Comparing and Contrasting	http://youtu.be/2kWY56sEJ5E
7	Focus Lesson, Grade 5: Citing Text Evidence	http://youtu.be/VTXkwvTCjsI
8	Discussion, Grade 5: Communication Skills	http://youtu.be/iZ5kjInK2SE
9	Focus Lesson, Grade 4: Grand Conversation	http://youtu.be/FZMgdE0s1CY
10	Discussion, Grade 6: Asking Good Questions	http://youtu.be/UaMS17SHmqI

	Description	Link
11	Discussion, Grade 6: Big Ideas	http://youtu.be/LKPdtJXufX4
12	Discussion, Grade 7: Vocabulary	http://youtu.be/gAqcKZUcu40
13	Fishbowl Discussion, Grade 9: Citing Evidence	http://youtu.be/K4qFFIqiKCg
14	Social Studies, Grade 9	http://youtu.be/_TZf3C4u3sM
15	Science, Grade 7	http://youtu.be/YsqyoJ_1XY8

Acknowledgments

I wish to thank the teachers listed below for allowing me to record them and their students as they worked on student-led discussions. Without their assistance, we would not have visual representations of some key components described in this publication. I also want to thank Principal Renee Brandner for supporting this project in her school.

- Cara Slattery – Teacher, Grade 6
- Cheryl Dueffert – Teacher, Grade 2
- Anne Haes – Teacher, Grade 1
- Lisa Swanson – Teacher, Grade 5
- Kelly Bridge – Teacher, Grade 4
- Heather Nemeth – Language Arts Teacher, Grade 7
- Danielle Christy – Language Arts Teacher, Grade 9

- Kevin Silberman – Social Studies Teacher, Grade 9
- Jill Gysberg – Science Teacher, Grade 9

References

Allington, R. L. (2001). *What really matters for struggling readers: Designing research-based programs.* Toronto: Addison-Wesley.

Allington, R. L., & Gabriel, R. E. (2012). Every child, every day. *Educational Leadership. 69*(8), 10–15.

Bakhtin, M. M. (1986). The Problem of Speech Genres. In *Speech genres and other late essays.* Austin: University of Texas Press.

Certo, J. L., Cualey, K. M., Moxley, K. D., & Chafin, C. (2008). An argument for authenticity: Adolescents' perspectives on standards-based reform. *The High School Journal. 91*(4), 26–39.

Daniels, H. (2002). *Literature circles: Voice and choice in book clubs and reading groups.* Portland, ME: Stenhouse.

Danielson, C. (2007). *Enhancing professional practice: A framework for teaching.* Alexandria, VA: ASCD.

Hammond, D. W., & Nessel, D. D. (2011). *The comprehension experience: Engaging readers through effective inquiry and discussion.* Portsmouth, NH: Heinemann.

Keene, E. O., & Zimmermann, S. (2007). *Mosiac of thought: The power of comprehension strategy instruction.* Portsmouth, NH: Heinemann.

Lent, R. C. (2012). *Overcoming textbook fatigue: 21st century tools to revitalize teaching and learning.* Alexandria, VA: ASCD.

Marzano, R. J., & Pickering, D. J. (2005). *Building academic vocabulary: Teacher's manual.* Alexandria, VA: ASCD.

National Institute of Child Health and Human Development. (2000). *Report of the National Reading Panel. Teaching children to read: An evidence-based assessment of the scientific research literature on reading and its implications for reading instruction.* Washington, D.C.: U.S. Government Printing Office.

Nystrand, M. (2006). Research on the role of classroom discourse as it affects reading comprehension. *Research in the Teaching of English, 40*(4): 392–412.

Pearson, P. D., & Gallagher, M. C. (1983). The instruction of reading comprehension. *Contemporary Educational Psychology, 8*(3), 317–344.

Shaskan, T. P., & Guerlais, G. (2011). *Honestly, Red Riding Hood was rotten: The story of Little Red Riding Hood as told by the wolf.* North Mankato, MN: Picture Window Press.

Thompson, C. L., & Zeuli, J. S. (1999). The frame and the tapestry: Standards-based reform and professional development. In L. Darling-Hammond & G. Sykes (Eds.). *Teaching as the learning profession: Handbook of policy and practice.* New York: Teachers College Press.

Zwiers, J., & Crawford, M. (2011). *Academic conversations: Classroom talk that fosters critical thinking and content understandings.* Portland, ME: Stenhouse.

About the Author

Sandi Novak has been a teacher, a principal (elementary and junior high), a curriculum director, and an assistant superintendent in Minnesota. She currently works as an educational consultant. She is married with three grown children and has two grandchildren that love to read.